I0418384

# HUSBAND MATERIAL VOL. II:
## TWENTY-SEVEN ADDRESSES

# D.L. HUSBAND

Photo by Chris Milburn (@chris.capturess)

Image editing by Shane Reilly
(@shanereillyartistofficial)

COPYRIGHT © D.L. Husband 2025

All rights reserved. No part of this publication may be reproduced or utilised in any form or by any means, electronic or mechanical, including photocopying, recording, all by any information storage and retrieval system, without permission in writing from the publishers.

ISBN 979-8-9913942-2-2

Published by Hidden Hand Press
www.hiddenhandbooks.com

HIDDEN HAND PRESS

*Husband Material Volume II:*

*Twenty-Seven Addresses*

*by D.L. Husband*

# CONTENTS

## Part Two: Screens and Pages

*Part Three: Pages That Move Me*

# PREFACE

Turns out, chaos can be controlled. Well, perhaps not controlled—
*harnessed.*

I grew worried that after taking a guttershark out of his natural environment and allowing some much needed time for healing from the wars and paranoid dark of the *deep deep deep* littered and polluted ocean that rolls away under all our feet, he might lose some of those sharp movements needed when hustling up a meal, or the sixth sense that allows anything to survive there, let alone get out.

But, in these calm and temperate waters, he finds a newfound sense of hope. The predatory mindset borne of those years addicted to destruction turn their sights on something more positive—more real. Now comes the time to hunt for his voice. His reason for hunting and hustling: to promote change.

Funny thing about it is, it's the same streets I now attempt to ply my new trade; sell my poetic wares. Never said I wasn't a *street* shark; I just wasn't a very good one. So, instead I settled down in a lonely cove I found with nourishing food for a developmental, philanthropic guttershark to heal, to ruminate. To remember what it was to *not* be something maligned and feared.

He needed a *new image*.

Setting feverishly about transformations on personal levels, abstaining from the meat (booze) to keep his keen edge sharper than ever. Thus, we find our protagonist well—hungry for more of all of this wonderful poetic existence he found after leaving that lonely but nurturing cove.

Back amongst the other urban sealife does he swim. On the same streets. With the same faces. Only now, he sees things so...much...differently.

Welcome to 'Husband Material Volume II: Twenty-seven Addresses.'

Enjoy

# Part One:

## That Which Moves; While We Move

So, whether you're back for more or with us for the first time, welcome. I write this tentatively, considering both message and meaning. Not just for this piece of writing with which I am about to share. Multiple pieces. My body of work, you could say. I'm body positive, you see. But how much of this body and what amount of myself I would offer up on the proverbial 'Aztec sacrificial slab' has troubled me. An antiquated metaphor or two is something I suggest you familiarise yourself with. Individual outlooks aside, we experience together.

"You've gotta *knaa* where you've been, to *knaa* where you're *gannin'*..." quoting someone smarter. Tends to be another continual human trend, being influenced by what we've heard and what we've seen, then recording it or orating it. History envies the future. The future just forgets...

It's hard to say something profound, especially something so concise and fat free as a single sentence quote. Feel if my literary endeavours were ever to be compared to the masters who came before, I'd be found wanting amongst good company who felt the same once, I'm sure. Firing and forging emotion, compulsion and experience. Firing and forging many masks and many swords.

With that being said, time after time I've found myself at the juxtaposition of feeling like the last person to offer advice, insight or comment. Yet, I was the one who was first to dish it out.

Never take it, mind you.

Now, here I am furiously tapping out words like I'd drink water after three days in the desert. Or a double voddy, and then three more. I'm a thirsty boy these days, ~~nine months sober~~. Seventeen days since my last accident.

Sobriety is not a straight line. I'm working on it.

But it is not only this thirst I work to quench...

I'm thirsty for more. Thirsty for better. To speak my poetic truth and hope it's not unwarranted. I know it's spent a long time being considered; facing the ruthless scrutiny that is me.

*'Pop culture fed both eagles and vultures. Spent my life feeling like she always had my number. In with the out crowd but always undercover. I don't know who I am. But I know my alternative culture like no other.'*

I wrote that in 2005. I've never fitted in, always felt like a shoe on the wrong foot but that's never really scared me. Though sometimes it does leave me feeling somewhat detached. An island alone, in a sea full of islands. A deaf tree in a forest full of constant, utopian communication.

Hard to describe, if you asked unnamed people, "He could've done so much if he hadn't...," they'd say they were there. They'd say they did as much as they could. But it's hard to agree and also know the truth.

None of it was simple. None of it was easy...I suppose nothing is.

Some people will understand that, some won't. Fair fucks. All I do know is that, for all the negative situations—

*I remain forever positive.*

Some of the things that have always brought me joy are the words of others. Be it on the silver screen, on well-read and worn pages, dropped over a banger or delivered through the technology which I write it on.

You can learn so much if you let it in. Really *hear* it, you know. These pieces which I share with you here are a homage to others' words and stories; characters played and characters written. They have helped me deal with my own mental health struggles. Writing, reading, and sharing. I still suffer, some days are so much harder than others—fluctuations in mood and mind.

Things that move; while we move.

## BEEN STRUGGLING

Been struggling to sleep,

Been struggling to read.

Been struggling to write,

Been struggling to breathe.

Have I really lost my countenance? Afflicted by some cruel disease.

If I could find a Lord which I could trust, on bended knee I'd plead...

"Help me All Father! Mother Gaia, I beseech! Please help me find the words that hang tantalisingly out of reach."

Before, just like the times 'afore I was thrown headlong into the breach.

I was owed the world that was sold to me, not this treacherous deceit.

Been struggling to live,

Been struggling to love.

Been struggling to understand,

Been struggling with me.

# WEATHERING IT

Was this all pre-ordained? Every special piece of pain, slotted into place to make a person whole again? Amidst torrential rains whipping over the bleak moors of a soul. It isn't always the sunshine that makes you sane.

Allow the storm to cleanse and wash the body of dirt and dust, from living as we do. Thunder rattles through the mind clearing away the debris. Lightning flashes, lighting up the way, giving vision to really see. That in the gloom and dreary darkness, there lives a little bit of me.

A search for the body continued into the day after next. No sign or trace of those that were lost that night. It left the investigators vexed. Searching in vain for any skeletal remains but they will find naught and abort, cold case closed and the report said the night simply swallowed them.

But those of us that weathered that squall, embraced it as a lover. Allowed it to strip us of our earthly camouflage and cover. Standing naked in awe of the brutal beauty of it all. We're not all reborn in flames. Some of us crawl back up, out of the deluge and its cataclysmic, all-consuming rage.

## SOMETIMES HEARTS

Sometimes hearts are surrounded by a kaleidoscope of butterflies. Other times, they are fortified with many feet of steel and stone.

Some hearts are surrounded by untended gardens, unkempt and overgrown. Some are frozen in barren tundra, the permanence of perma-loss and snow.

Some hearts are surrounded by innumerable bodies, feasting on new love's forlorn glow. Some simply beat through each day, rhythmic monogamy, pumping away.

Some hearts are surrounded by shrapnel, love terrorism is here to stay. Some are full of wondrous, enviable joy, never touched by abject dismay.

Some hearts are surrounded by plastic and never get a chance to start. Some are beating so weak, you barely hear them depart.

Some hearts are surrounded by so many ghosts, Bill Murray wouldn't know where to start. Some are twisted chunks of blistered meat, seared on the coals of distinct, devouring hate.

Some hearts are surrounded by second chances, second interviews and second dates. Some fall short of the mark, never gaining back trust, letting go, rejection and dejection their eternal mates.

Some hearts are surrounded by laughter, put back together with clown illustration covered plasters. Some never came back from war, lost *on/to* an unnamed shore. Lost to the sea, Lost where they fall.

Some hearts are surrounded by damaged bodily tissue, corrective scarring causing real issues. Some beat a single snare drum in bed, as last breaths are shed, the drummer finally gets to rest.


Let your heart live, before it's dead.

# SORROWFUL SYNERGY

Why is he so broken? Maybe, just maybe, he can't ever be fixed. Juxtaposed between caring too much and never giving a shit. Uses white hot wit combined with years of hiding it. 'It' being the incredible weight, the heartbreak and beautiful dread it is to really love, and truly co-exist.

Amorphous feelings overwhelm. Sorrow claiming squatters' rights in my aorta; until its empathic eviction, there it dwells. Good intentions paved the rocky road to my own personally manifested hell. The vessel is sinking and the captain's left the helm. Been way too long since both boy and man felt even close to being well.

Synaptic synergy abounds between myself and misery. We hold hands and we slip away. Perhaps forever, immovable, unrelenting weight, of this horrible history. Into the water I fall—gracefully and gratefully, sinking deep, dancing the dead man's tango with my heart made of stone and my feet of clay. They broke the only mould and left me this way.

How can one survive the storm when they *are* the fucking storm? Rattling familial windowpanes and blowing in doors that bonds had opened in times before. Creating chaos categorically: like it or not, you will respect my authority. I was born amidst the tempest's dishonesty. Perhaps, it's impossible to reform.

*I can't be an anomaly.*

Consumed by capricious, combustible thoughts, burned at the pyre for the incantations that I wrought. Cursed in name, cursed the shame, cursed the lack of self belief and cursed the cutting, cursory blame. Cursed and cursed—black magic shaken on the rocks with my disdain. Martini glassed the last warlock who tried to disarm me of my final fuck, give no quarter—self-represent your precious pain, still the boiling waters, sharpen your diction and sharpen your blade, old habits hide to escape the predicted, tumultuous slaughter I bade.

*Oh, behave!*

Adorned in my cantankerous cowl; scowl gives way to my hallowed howl. For this pain I'm responsible. For this hurt I'm responsible. Monstrous intent, mediocrity is so close to me. Admonished and abominable, future failures causing my insomnia. I'd take it easy if the words didn't displease me. Heart's been set to self-destruct; lost so many rounds I've got *nowt* left but a rotten liar's luck.

Feelings left in the barbed wire to bleed, they make for good target practice, a mile marker just for me. One day, I'll storm the trenches of my discontent—bayonet what's left, hopelessly bereft. Maybe one day I'll win the war against really being me.

# SEDIMENTARY CLUTTER

Here's a little diatribe: could I have died for my tribe? Spear in hand, Stone Age garb, trying not to get eaten alive. Seems to me there's a soliloquy that the past and future always utter... "Try and survive us both...if you dare".

Perhaps you'd find both our bones like old sedimentary clutter.

Sometimes they shout, sometimes they mutter. But never do they ever stutter or splutter. They speak words that cut, like this Jabberwocky's Vorpal blade—often wondered if they pondered the same question as me:

"Can I survive this life?"

Sometimes quite literally.

We may finish the race early, but our race will keep on living. Gather those around you, light the fire, share some food and experience neolithic giving; when the catch of the day is having that day your own way, I've found myself so much more forgiving. Exile yourself from that tribe and you face the world alone, learning ancient lessons.

Maybe we die out in the wild under stars. Or we make it back in one piece although we barely survived! Tell our story while the flames roar—of monsters faced and foes vanquished. Like them, I bring back the head of the beast to show my trial's complete. They return to their tribe with skills and with meat. We've both got stories but the fresh kills that I present to you all are my past and future sober weeks.

# BORDER WAR

Grey and dormant:

horizon fights an unsteady border war with water.

Such a depth of blue green ocean.

Sea foam washing around bare feet:

poetry in motion,

could just as easily wash away all there is to see.

The briny deep before the man holds up a mirror to his briny depression.

Second-guessing upcoming events order of procession.

Possession with intention, court-mandated intervention.

Under water, feeling smaller.

Drowning in the shallows, losing focus while swallowing temptations for sensations.


Drowning in the shallows.

_d r o w n i n g_

# FRAGILE—HANDLE WITH CARE

Spoon-feed me pain—tantalisingly delectable tidbits to keep up the needed levels of insane. Something I know how to consume. Gaining nothing but days, spent in the dumps of my mind's back lanes, claws retract at corners as they are approached, is it the fear and melancholy that are the substitutes for being sane?

Classically educated in feeling left out, feeling let down, feeling absolutely fucking *nowt*—

Liar—

*Pants on fire*—

You live with an all-consuming doubt/shame/rage/blame game, set and match. Patching up wounds with 'let's make amends', although you can't mend what was broken because you'll likely just break it again.

Fragile—handle with care is the handle you hope will start to trend—hashtag break one more time before you descend.

But when you're abrasive, flammable and invasive like a nitroglycerine and kerosene-soaked sandpaper wrap for the blade of the guillotine; how the fuck can anyone safely operate or execute when beneath is a black hole singularity you've come to know as who you are—

who you *must* be?

Job's fucked and you know it. Unless you can find a way
to slow it

d

o

w

n

on the mental,

this overwhelming doom is fifty shades of detrimental.

Can't do it to them. Perhaps, you just do it to ~~you~~ me.

Endeavouring to disgorge an all encompassing expulsion,

Exorcising corruption of flesh and pathos bred of ego,
bravado, lethargy and disastrous assumption.

Seduction by the demonic darkness is a constant—

revealing truth in the presumption:

that no one cares even though they say they do.

# THE MOON WATCHES ON

The moon watches on.

She watches *wars* waged. She watches bombs and explosions; land grab light shows. Rolling, rumbling progress, cost counted in bones and wasted protest.

She watches *controlled* burns. She watches once abundant, lush green; kerosene-kissed rainforest recession. Fiery, smoking progress, cost counted in pollution and wasted protest.

She watches *overflowing* oceans. She watches rubbish dumped and sealife eradication; plastic continents replace ice. Packaged, polystyrene progress, cost counted in ecological disasters and wasted protest.

She watches the *absence* of gods. She watches churches razed and wasted prayers; abandoned sycophantic deity botherers. Bloody, intolerant progress counted in gold by backward doG(s) and wasted protest.

Old mother moon; marooned. A celestial personified chameleon—Silver-tongued or yellow-bellied, blue-faced or bristling red. Watching, waiting as only tidally-locked lovers wait: until the end of time.

Many other lonely cosmic travellers have passed her. Some stop to say hello, leaving real impacts on her.

Some hurtle by, tails wagging for thousands of years. Some hit the next best thing, her unexpecting dance partner, Earth. Only the oldest rocks manage mirth correctly.

Reset. Fifteen thousand years. Reset. Triceratops? Reset. Tyrannosaurus R-reset! For time measured in galaxies rolled off a series of complex        construction lines with many elements and a team of quantum entangled architects putting out masterpiece after masterpiece.

Heterogenous giant furnaces and super dense solar displays blasting galactic extermination rays. That Jimmy Neutron kid has some serious gravitational pull and raw, untamed star power, so the moon tells the story, anyway.

From a god's eye view: all-consuming super black predators, they say all goes down the drain anyway; stands to reason. All matter is circling the banqueting black: even the hole perhaps implodes when it has eaten all the cosmic table scraps. Will they feed on each other; then allofeed in a never ending wynorrific display of infinite, repetitious power? All that regurgitated molecular promise; beautiful flakes of noble atomic feed.

Produced behind the curtain; just out of sight. Observables aside, all is bound by vibration and gravity. Macroscope for discovery is breaking the fourth wall, revealing particles behaving oddly; mysterious mammals masturbating over explicit millisecond-long clips of creation's micro-machinery.

He watches on—

As the moon sinks into a hungry horizon, a deflated, broken heart sinks with her.

Without more understanding, his cycle remains in finite, fragile motion.

*Part Two:*

*Screens and Pages*

All this paginated dreaming is keeping me up at night.

Not so bad, given what used to delay (or indeed altogether postpone) my trips to dreamtown. Stresses of the mind and trouble at the door. Messy environments breed messy habits. Crazy can only take you so far, then, it begins to require some focus, some organisation; one may say, *finesse*.

But marrying that up with form and structure, lacking in any classical education and an aversion to rules could have been my undoing, stopped this literal literary foray dead in its presumptuous tracks. This is, alas, where I must stick to my uncultured guns and sew my own seeds, see what ideas may grow.

In this and my first collection, I use pieces spanning over ten years of writing. So much was lost along the way but

*such is life.*

In the last collection, I told my story (in condensed form). In this one, I hope to shed some light on the influences and growth, in myself and others. Change is ever present. We see this more than ever in the chaotic world around us, in the lives we have lived, seen lived, or maybe more often, *not* lived. Where *we* came from, where *we're* going, knowing history and *your* history holds the key.

Thinking more about what went into making these words I write in earnest, has me dwelling on a line I heard in *The Gentleman* (TV show) by Guy Ritchie when used in description of the Edwardian architect and creative force William Kent "feral meets refined". In so many ways, I live for these words. They more aptly describe how I wrap up myself, levels and levels of synchronicity with three little words.

Certainly not the only important three-word phrase, that is for sure. Short sentences, properly punctuated and carefully considered carry a weight all their own.

I love you.

We've missed you.

She lost him.

Flourishing and flowery vocabulary peppering metaphor is one thing. But those short statements are heavy with suggestions and questions—intrigue.


Less is more. It's a secret. Page and Screen.

On we go...

## RING OF FIRE

I am bound upon a wheel of fire—

Burn, burn, burn,     so it goes.     The man in black
is tantalised.     Tantalus' cabinet just within reach
feeling like Autolycus stole the cattle...

    *Yet,*


    we carve upon the calfs made heifers so they may
never be stolen again. Crosses branded on calendars
again. We move against the gods *because* we are men.

    Our *inability to submit and ability to trick*


    May find us pushing the prophetic boulder
*but that should never remove your reason to resist.*


It's your reason to exist...

## ZOMBIE FEELINGS

Zombie feelings.

                         Left me    r  e  e  l  i  n  g.

Way easier to h a c k them apart than ever deal with
dealing.

Headshots will do nicely, ideas and brain matter all *owa*
the ceiling.

It's displeasing how many of these undead emotions are
around, diseased and in need of feeding.


*Groovy—*


I just found a best friend.

Time to crank up the chainsaw; Ash has found the book
of the dead. Sometimes flesh is the price when it's 'horde
mode' on nightmare internally.

But don't get so surly, there could always be a cure. It's
just too early to be sure. The *Evil Dead* can be banished
amidst much introspective gore.

So, for now let's get back to beating that high score.

Killed a million zombie feelings, really hope they were all sick.

If not, that must make me genocidal against *what*

I

      **really**

**think.**

## REAPER MAN

Lonely soldier walking slowly, only you know where the ghosts will be. Or the enemies, iron love at first sight, the foliage disguising them changing elevation by degrees.

Wounds fill tombs. Answering the cryptkeeper— another forever sleeper in the boneyard of the reaper. Lurking life-taker, brown bread baker. Emaciation or incarceration, gas chamber or hard labour.

Lonely older passing the graves of the soldier, murals on walls for the fallen taken in by the beholder. Of life in a pre-owned skeleton, rented and returned like it needs a receipt. Many give up themselves or accidentally replace their marrow back on the shelves—time runs out, deceitful as ever...

> *Time's cunning that way—*
> *you always think you have more.*

Cold follows the dead. Full moons illuminate headstones, but those burned or drowned, eaten or dissolved perhaps don't get to shake hands on the forever sands with MORT.

So, when it's the time, Reaper Man, play that sweet Soul Music, remove the timer from the shelf and make my words—my mausoleum.

From Small Gods to hell's gates.

## BLAMELESS BLAGGARD

With drugs comes crime and when I was in my prime,
I'd be lining 'em up, awake every night, considering
where the money could be. Worrying about enemies
both seen and unseen. In the dirty streets, monsters exist
and they feed on your dreams. They cling to you with
talons that scratch and sink rotten teeth proper deep.
Drag you down to the bottom and there you shall
remain. Lost your home so long ago, you're not from
whence you came.

That blameless blaggard was becoming pretty haggard.
His bacon was cooked. Race ran, he was paggered. The
time had come to get off the beaten track and circle up
the wagons. Threats flooded down from the road ahead
and sharpshooters sent it from the ridge. Spaghetti
western references aside, we all know fighting for our
lives from a gang of destructive intentions.

Survived the last attack but I know they'll be back.
Travel light—time to mosey on, best get moving.
Looking over my shoulder for days, travelled miles out
of the way. Still in the distance, I feel pursuers and they
grow closer judging by the cloud of dust. Horses strain
under stress and running hard through the night. No
time for food or water or praise. In that moment, she

gave up and bucked me from the saddle. Went down never to move again.

Recuperation from new injuries ain't even the slimmest pipedream for me. Get to unsteady feet, body filled with untempered red-hot aggression. I take cover behind my fallen steed denying the scavengers their feast. Got two bullets left. One for me, not before I give the first one to the leader. I wait in pain, mud, shit and rain. Then hoof beats announce their arrival. I raise my pistol and take aim.

Sweat beads on the brow but steady was the hand. They drew closer and I could see my tormentors. They all looked as one—a twisted figure made of smoke. Wearing identical clothing brandishing weapons used to threaten and extort. There in the lead was the largest, riding a demonic steed. Eyes filled with fire and with death looked my way and I unleashed my penultimate lead slug revenge.

Heard the bang, heard the horses snort. I'd closed my eyes as I pulled the trigger fearing not hearing the guns report. I open them up and see merely ghostly apparitions, fading away into atmospheric matter. Bleeding in the road lay the source of my discontent. Reconciliation can come later, the sky opens up and cries a solemn pitter patter. Off I head in search of riches and redemption, covered in my old life's bloody spatter.

# BUFFET

Inside the cauldron that boils my hurt and my hate, bubbles pop on its surface releasing the perfume of sulphur and rotten words. Rotten feelings and rotten luck.

Stir

Stir                        Stir

Stir                    Stir

Stir the pot, stir the shit, stir up all the memories of things that were said and that which we did. That which I did. The horror filled showreels of the nights when I hid from bone collectors and debt collectors. I collect my own scenes that I hold with such tragic affection. These ancient rooted afflictions make *constant* indecision the only decision.

Bubbling on the surface whilst the howling continues beneath. Salty tears fall onto hollow beliefs. Hallowed graves are dug up and brought forth from them are my reanimated kin.

Bubbling pot full of my ghastly gruel to serve to my kindred spirits. Doesn't need proof, there won't be any pudding. The corpses of who I was keep on nodding to the melancholy music. Memories of abuse continue abusing, memories of loss are all I keep finding. Dirt beneath broken nails, lies behind broken teeth. A heart that has turned to stone and shattered to shards becomes the shroud for what has withered yet remains beneath.

They orbit this grief as if gravitationally bound. Bound to me. Bound to who I am and all that I can ever be.

Stewed on how to serve this dish for years.

*Whose deigned palate will this satisfy?*

How many other broken people pass up on this buffet that I've made from parts of me?

## ANANKE

Ananke rules in my palacial psyche—

I pray and render both living and burnt offerings.

Offering up vestiges—pieces of who I used to be     still
born being forlorn and unable to connect insight to
feeling, seeing to believing.

The pen and this addiction co-mingle just as Ananke and
Chronus entwine in serpentine ways around the cosmos.

Do the Moirai and the mindful fates have my thread
spun upon their wheel?

Does necessity embody me?

Is it the condemnation that I truly seek?

Relinquishing control to the chaos and the light to the
dark—character arcs.

Superstition. Prejudice. Elements.

This church will always face its dogma, this creation will
always face its laws, this plough and this ship will always
face frozen ground and the intrepid sea.

This triple Ananke weighs upon us all.

This triple Ananke swells within me.

# DEMOLITION MAN

Demolition man. A created constellation etched in a psilocybin-hallucination showreel.

He's here to fuck up future plans. Rebuild the past on scorched earth with mass grave foundations made to last.

*"Then you were nice enough to wake me up and let me know everything that meant something in my life is gone. It would've been more humane to stake me down and leave me to the fucking crows."*

Imagine how the crow felt—Hollywood reclaiming myth misrepresenting stories.

Apollo blackened feathers for dissent—the humours are in a permanent imbalance.

Stallone mirroring a morose sentiment awoken from the cryo sleep, will feeling and seeing – passenger-seat dreaming – addiction and desperation steering – sniping and pipes and window peeping – fist-clenching anxiety-ridden cleaning – dispassion and overwhelming intoxicated then

impassioned and furious

necessitous—

exaggerated ways of being.

Dopamine nose bags leading to ice cracking or the craggy     scabby     skaglands.

Peck, peck, peck, peck, peck, peck, peck, fucking peck.

Doomed. Last breath. Burnt tin foil and blackened spoons. Hypodermic debris. Could've done it and lived spartan, lean and warlike against anything and who we used to be. It wasn't to be. It was never really me.

Never be a non-smoker. Never be a non-drinker. Never be a non-top set class A, B and C through Z drug taker.

*Can't ever be that*

*when you've done it too much.*

*" Give me three vowels and four consonants Carol, if you please."*

You're only an ex- of anything when you're addicted to it.

That's the crux of addictions—alphabetti spaghetti.

Too many combinations to alleviate a myriad of momentary discomforts and emotional pain behaving capriciously inside.

## ALL NAPOLEON, NO DYNAMITE

All about that hard work. All about the grind. Searched so long, I swear my eyes were sore and madness sent me blind. Found what I was looking for on its perpetual decline. Now I work out my work ethic all the time, only me pockets getting lined.

Guilty of *nowt* as it's always no comment. Less you say, the more you know. Easy to spot a plot, avoid brain damage and blood clots. Just drink your fucking drink little man. Eat your tater tots.

All Napoleon, No dynamite. Five foot four and a great tactician. Left decimation everywhere I went marching on like a single man division. Bet my blow up will be less TNT, more like the bombing of Dresden. Slaughterhouse five on a live stream.

Could've easily been me. John Doe no identity, fished out of the Tyne after a handful of weeks. Owed the fucking lot out all the time, more ticky than a broken clock. Had me doing desperate things when I was feeling *nowt* but meek. If you're ever pushed right to your limit you'll know just how far you'd go. Gotta say my outlook was *canny* bleak.

Packed the whole game in and threw it away. Thought it was the only one I knew how to play. Sure, we played each other but that was the way. It was time to leave snow to Santa and to sleighs. Turn over a new leaf each time I fill another page. Realised that working my pen and my herb are the best way to avoid the cage.

I'm not here chatting shit, just trying to avoid the abyss. Spent years more than staring into it, gave it a full-on sloppy kiss. It kissed me back. Made me relax. Kick off ya shoes and hit it from the back. Then when you're not watching... *fuck*, where's my life at?

The abyss mate, you took the piss mate. No one thought you were coming back. But back I fucking am. Burning brighter than ever. Got really tasty in there for a hot minute but now I'm finally back off the session. Order has for once been restored. Manning up really was a blessing. Now I'm caressing these words, they're undressing, thinking, "Is he all talk, or could he really teach me a lesson?"

*Eyebrows, eyebrows....*

## FAIRY TRIALS

In your world, Incy Wincey spider climbed up the water spout. In mine two cons climb up ya drainpipe to burglarise ya house. Creeping about, no water coming down to wash these intrusive arachnids out.

Only the blues and twos will clear ransacked, darkened rooms. Either they'll get out or they'll *gan* with *nowt*. Old Mother Hubbard's got *nowt* left in the cupboard; they've even had the silverware out of the sideboard. Booted in the door to her boot, looking for a score. Blame us, blame us: the bored, addicted lost and the societally ignored.

Will they steal our dreams? Neglected social welfare systems and the NHS has suffered the most, picked apart at the seams. The state of this nouveau Britain has got me so sick I'm seething and spitting.

Wee Willy Winky, always a little tipsy. Never mind the candlestick he's got a one point five of whisky. Lifting up his nightgown when he's growing and he's frisky. Tick tock, the rat ran up the clock, tick tock red door key unlocks—an early morning trip to the copper shop. Owld Georgie Porgy got the pudding and the pie, but paid the crust out to stave off a beating for bills he tried to flout. Surprise, surprise.

Little Red Riding Hoody, riding bikes around the neighbourhood-y, robbing purses, bags, phones, man she's got all them stolen goodies. Maybe we shouldn't but we always should-y...

Nursery rhymes spun from the yarn from the bottom rung of the ladder. Bottom rung of the ladder.

Ain't much left that makes me sadder...

## Twenty-Seven Addresses

Rumination on ruination; wretched redemptive inclination towards postulating and fabricating (in other words, fake it    u n t i l you make it). Not for *OnlyFans* of fiction; birthed from a severe concrete addiction: a story of gutters and rats, of this, and of that. Of names made up in a supposed black book that allegedly contained twenty-seven addresses.

While we've ascertained the story's fake, here's the real talk:

How about this work addresses you twenty-seven times? Clear lessons—words from the prisoner in the page, be it an A4 cage or the digital box. He is a sage and at this stage you need to listen, how else will you learn what to do?

1.      If you're going to say it, make it loud and proud. Even sorrow can be expressed with dignity when you're sleeping on cold ground.

2.      Unless they're names and you are playing *that kind* of game...in that case, zzzzzzzip the lips and don't admit to shit.

3.      No comment, solicitor. Listen and know what is good for ya. Speak your truth in indecision, next thing ya banged up in more than one self made prison.

4.      If that happens, do the time, learn and remind, that there is a life after this and you can still really make something of it.

5.      Pay your bills on time when they're owed round the doors, those scores get sky high. Chores become choring and broken glass on floors.

6.      Don't take more than you can manage; borrowing food from a hungry savage...might get you stuck in the teeth of a pack of predatory animals.

7.      If that happens, take the beating and learn the lesson. Pick the phone up. Someone suggested that to me before. He hadn't, he simply ignored, the volcanic vibration; call after call.

8.      Debt doesn't just disappear. It ends up in little books. In notes, in phones and in the mind's darker nooks. *Gan canny*, forgot to mention the crannies, basically, everywhere you go, some debts are *gannin'*.

9.      So, now you're not eating for three, suppose if you don't feed the voices they'll wither in defeat? *Wey* not likely. Keep *gannin'*, everytime you look in a mirror they start to feast.

10.    Peeping curtains and the constant calls and texts begin literally physically hurting. "I'm just running to the shops," becomes just that, a mad dash through rarely used paths, detours and three tours, seen people spend hours doing laps.

11.    Thought they'd be slick, in and out quick, then they hear the laughter of the grafter above, catch a glimpse and stop dead in their tracks.

12.    Attacks of PTSD during dinner service. Had the secret and the key. Shaking drinks while stimulant nerve spasms and body chemistry shook me. An actor acting like the actions at hand actually mattered at all.

13.    Turning points and sojourns become turning tables and one isn't stæegs away, stick the twist, win just one game of wist; it's a start, you're finally ticking things off the list.

14.    Hammer the work. Same attitude as grafting in the dirt. Spent years shirking responsibility— remember, the old ways always lurk.

15.    Clean the mirror you use to see yourself, I guarantee it's grimy. Clean yourself up, give it a little time. Remember the first day you shone again between hurt and hard graft.

16.    Now, also *divvn't* kid yourself, you're still just a shit-smeared rough cut. Not fit for a princess, cut from

the same cloth. But now you know what you are, you could dare to suggest a tryst.

17.     Wit is something you best learn to keep well in your remit. Life is happy and sad, but those around you will be glad when you can laugh through grief and hardship, never again taint yourself and submit.

18.     Love's a lock with a philosophical key. Another thing that's never clean. But purer than *owt* you'd get on the streets.

19.     Don't bash it, enjoy it while it lasts. Know it comes with a hook that is always cast. I've done pretty much every drug under the sun, true love is still the most powerful one.

20.     Challenge yourself to be better, than an unironed fucking sweater, shirt creased up and covered; sweat-stained pits sprayed, on the way out the door kicking aside unopened letters.

21.     Don't be late for those appointments you made. Time matters to others even if you don't care quite the same.

22.     Be kinder. Discussed in a publication as a constant reminder. Damage done, wars lost and won. My embittered relationship with tenderness serves as a constant.

23.     Don't hate what you've become. Hate what you became. Chances for change come like rain, ignoring downpours doesn't have to be the way.

24.     Believe the words that come with no presupposition, admission that some people can make truthful statements and decisions, to be good, to speak truth, to take you under the wing or take the time to soothe. See through the grime and the person you both knew.

25.     *Divvn't* kid the *kidder* in the mirror. The cave and shadow serpents will always have venom to deliver. Keep you inside away from the world, frozen microwave dinners. But eating alone when you've more than just a dog, you've got a bone. Chopped-up life isn't just chopped liver.

26.     You can't change what has come to pass. You can react though, no matter how recalcitrant. That's your choice. In your voice. You just need to keep saying it, man.

27.     The last lesson. Whether it's all gone or whatever. Don't give up on yourself. Not ever. Forever is a *long* fucking time.

## GHOSTBUSTERS

Spent a lot of time dining with hungry ghosts.

Spirits seeking nourishment from that which matters the most.

Fridge left open, light left on, several I.O.U. notes.

Ghastly retainers on paper for the remainder of my persona. Grand, ghoulish gesticulators pretending to eat a hodge podge leftover feast, picking at the bones of their god and creator.

Spent a lot of time living with hungry ghosts.

Spectres stranded and trapped in rooms. They maintain their posthumous posts.

Left akimbo, in limbo, some beg and some boast.

Spooky marauders in places remembered or avoided. Ethereal entities enveloping these rooms in fear and fright. Apparitions wrapped in the horror of past decisions, situations, trials and tribulations. In their sheets, past pain and trauma is embroidered.

Spent a lot of time sleeping with hungry ghosts.

Sexual encounters with spectral exhibitionists.

Voyeuristic wraiths watching on, belittling kingmakers.

Phantasms fornicate in candid, illicit memories in imagined places, with imagined faces. Decadent, destructive dreams in the darkness with seductive, salacious shades. Old flames sidle on, garter-belted eidolons, ideals are gone with the absence of the sun. Hallowed ground haunted with historic harlots and devilish, distorted passionate sounds.

Like Venkman and Spengler, spangled by the vortex. The streams crossed. The gatekeeper won. Zuul will rule, zealously cruel.

There Gozer neighbourhood.

I am the Gozerian.

# SQUID (WORD)

Caught between Scylla and Carybdis.

Familiar rocks and hard places cause oceanic pressures.

The depth of the character required leads to and through where REAL monsters swim.

In this abysmal abyss, abyssal gigantism is the phenomena one needs to sustain.

Feeding on feelings—tentacles feeling out in the lonely, roaring silence. I always found the permanent dark so cold and so inviting.

Fleeing prey brushes against scarred and pockmarked organic fishing lines. Wrapped up; gripped by sucking, hook-hiding suckers.

Pulled into a flurry of roiling, grasping arms. Seeking to feed this abyssal, abysmal beast. Broken beak from battles bygone, sinks into flesh of bottom-feeding emotions. Hunger retreats and the briny deeps isolating pain

fleets...

Chummed water in the darkness back-lit by bioluminescence.

Photophyre headlights provide precision for gripping suction. Distance-judging, stereoscopic sight needed for abyssal hunting.

The waters have calmed around this cancerous cephalopod. Short bursts of frenzied fury catching those that lost their way in the black.

Gladius-clad gladiatorial gargantuan combatant, colossus of the colossal calamari Kings reigns supreme in the fathomless coliseum.

Mantle-propelled past breaks in the bottom's facade revealing mantle. *Luminescent* ink sprays, blinding predators; two hearts working fast to evade the whale's chase.

Chromatophores flash. The beast sinks back into the murky black. There, apparently dormant, it will wait. Tendrils seeking for prey that descend from the sunlit surface track.

An ocean swells beneath this skin. With many a beast to feast on misplaced feelings.

*Architeuthis Dux:* Read 'The Beast' and found reflection redux.

*Part Three:*

*Pages That Move Me*

No one gets out clean. You are just cleaner than you were. Good thing about being a shark is the waters you live in wash away the blood and gore of the last feeding frenzy and leave you unstained. But you're not clean, never ever again. The scars will always be there. The scars, visible or invisible, both as indelibly etched into you as if chiseled in stone. I'm learning to live with it. Still my favourite suit to wear, this one made of meat that belongs to me.

Couldn't throw away old clothes, but throwing away old habits seems easier. NOT easy. Let's not get ahead of ourselves. This has been a hard fucking slough. Every day comes with temptation: beckoning with libations and intoxication. It has dwindled somewhat, control has been exerted but I'd be lying like print if I didn't admit that most days remain fragile like bone china in clumsy hands—constantly under threat. Some days, the wire is breached. Those days though, are few and far between. Security is good and I run a tight ship.

The further through this work I get, the more I begin to realise it is as much about words and pages, screens and stages as it is about mental health, or the lack thereof. I am both cursed and imbued with anxiety, post-traumatic stress disorder and ADHD. This leaves me visiting dark places regularly and verily. Rarely do I manage to string more than a few days together without peering back into the darkness. This is another habit I am working hard to break. Hopefully with a few new forms of intervention, we might manage to see some change here. Though, would I swap all these words for it? I'm not sure, being honest.

Sobriety doesn't speak to me, naturally. I've always been more of a hellraiser. I hear the call in the wee hours, most of all. I'm up again wet nursing the demons I raise inside; incubating and hatching them anew. My creativity has always suckled at the many manifested teats of chaos. 'Bad' inspires just as much as 'good' does. My life has always motivated me ruthlessly—moved me with necessity. Survival or starvation. Get the bill paid or get broken bones and brayed. We should never try to quantify desperation when it enters the equation. It trumps most other feelings hands down.

But, as a reformed shark, making his way in the literary pools in which he now skirts...a different kind of desperation sets in. Well, perhaps desperation is not the best word, maybe *challenge* is more accurate. Challenged to be better than he is by recording these words, a testament to promises made and a check for future slips in nature and returning to the old beast. It has happened. He never said *forever*. But for now, responsibility is what he aims for, in all things in this life.

These are a selection of pages that have particularly moved me or have a special place in my heart, for this reason or that. Perhaps, you may glean why they matter to me. If you have panned enough literary river water to find those tiny flecks of gold that indicate you've tapped into a vein of precious, valuable, elemental *understanding*. If you have, kudos. If you know me, you will know why. If not, enjoy these final pieces I have chosen, carefully, from my own words. I hope they resonate in some way with *you*...

## DUSTBINS (AND OTHER SINS)

Rows of plastic, gluttonous figures line this lonely
alley—*dustbins* (and other sins): litter in, litter out.

Tonight must be that night. Time to take out the trash.
Oh, if only it were so easy.

It is strewn everywhere—too much for a team of
fluorescent coats and grabber sticks to ever (ever) clean
up.

Down *wor* way we're paid the alu-minimum wage.
Collected or rejected; ring pulls run rings around their
painted metal dungeon.

The discarded roses tin. In another house, in another
time (I hear the buttons, jangling)

Plastic. Plastic. *Plastic*. More and more and more.
Choking up this dank back lane ecosystem. Necessitous
and everywhere. Clogging up millions of minds. It lies
and says it will go away.

       Never believe it; garbage learns to trust its gut.

Scraps for the rats: at least they get to eat. It might not
be a feast but there's food to be had on this dirty street.

The leftovers. In another house, in another time (I hear
knives scraping plates, sharing).

Peels and flakes of debris—so many, many misbegotten motes. Perhaps, given a life they may have had dreams.

Colourful individual hues slowly decay into mulch... but, what's this? They grow something (batteries in the wrong bin).

Life growing technology. Technology poisoning cultural compost due to ignorance and complacency.

The springtime planting. In another garden, in another time (I smell fresh compost and flora: life).

Recycled with care; most things from the back roads will be useful again:turned into containers or absorbers again. Turned into canvas or frame.

Turned into something real, with purpose! Something people need again.

Summer evening party. In another garden, in another time (I smell family and petrichor: worth).

Thursday morn. Metal beasts with hydraulic jaws and more underpaid fluorescent spectres get their fill; clearing away compartmentalised detritus. Some will return, useful and find fulfilment. Others will not be so lucky.

It's rubbish, *being trash.*

Some *empty packet carcasses* and flat (once effervescent) dregs remain in transparent plastic (deflated) prisons.

Rows of plastic, bulimic figures compelled to expulsion. *Dustbins* (and other sins)—constant, catastrophic *consumption.*

## WHEN SEPTEMBER ENDS

Wake me up, when September ends—

to the auburn and burnt yellows of October; autumnal
camouflage pavements. Air thick with the drizzle's film
and a chance to burn the dead, beneath the witching
moon.

New romance enters a new lunar phase; longing for love
becomes a longer love as the seasons continue.

We both feel this way. We both know why. Those reasons
we share

*But*

*we*

*could **never** properly share.*

*We only hope for the strength*

*to*

*really,*

*properly care—to carry ourselves*
*through what remains in the ninth circle of the year;*

*remembering.*

Sunny—Green Days: before dismay:

give way to this month which feels like a year.

Encourages and seeks out tear ducts – overburdens the waterways requiring regular maintenance and testing of the water works.

The most painful passing of the calendar promotes both new and old hurt.

 Gone. They just remain so **irreplaceably**   fucking gone.

*Wake us up—*

*when September ends…*

# INDOOR MARKET MENTALITY

Indoor markets are magical places, fantasy lands filled with nic-nacs on plastic tables.

Smells waft across awnings from appealing hot treats—just in time, could really do with a bite to eat!

The critters and humans all remind me of each other, a strange sort...all salt of the earth, I'm sure.

However, they look as though they've been kicked through charity shops. Most must've been forever poor.

Can get everything you fancy in here: faux flowers for faux valentines, DIY products for the ever present need to repair.

Papers and bongs, radios playing poor covers of popular songs. Gun shops and sweet shops, tobacconist and the butchers, all where they belong.

Incense and incensed pensioners remind of many wonderful days spent—searching for toys, books and guitar strings while hatching adolescent ploys.

# 3D Printed Dinosaur Bones

Feeling as authentic as 3D printed dinosaur bones.

Prohibitively prohibiting an opportunity for growth.

Digging up emotional fossils on the daily. Cracking open rocks in search of precious ore; hidden elemental metals to patch up a multitude of chinks in this faithful armour. The old ways, *the old wars* became such a soul destroying, laborious bore.

Feeling as authentic as 3D printed dinosaur bones.

Prohibitively prohibiting an opportunity to clear centuries of smoke; from burning places of worship and those buried in the sea. Older religions had pantheons of gods, not just war ones, ignorant and fuelled by profit and conflict. Perhaps they sit playing games, with dice roll control over humans with guns and bombs from planes; if they survive, they must reside in  the cradle of civilisation and the European east.

Excavating dangerous cavern systems eternally: internally: subconscious spelunking: stress testing self-deluded presumptions. The torch went out so many times; the Olympics would be cancelled. I'd need Persephone and Hekate to rescue me if I Artemis(s) the way back outty.

Feeling as authentic as one of a myriad of plastic goddesses: stickered and sold in a foreign flea market.

Prophetised prophetic prophet's propping up poor decision making and bad judgement. Why write all these books of rules pitched by well-meaning fools to well-meaning fools? Surely an act of (insert name here) would prove this in a much more final way.

Transactional confessionals between an overzealous sin machine through a man collared into being a microphone; to ignorant gods driven mad by innumerable prayers. They cut off their ears, Van Gogh was in vogue; keep the money, save the words. They've been and gone man.

Feeling as authentic as one of a myriad of plastic goddesses: stickered and sold in foreign flea markets.

Prophetised prophetic prophets propping up sales and performing miracles, hoarding real estate; tax exempt temples with ledgers and tabs. Gone from organs in jars and sarcophagi to brimming mass graves and zip tied hands.

Actual battle rages in adjacent holy dirt. Increasing sales of metal beasts with grave digging teeth to store the dead; operated. collected and mourned by those who carry these religious wars body count and hurt. Why are there not wars in heaven over who's the godliness god, instead of on patches of earth? Humane thinkers know that these conflicts need to end...suppose Godzilla and Mothra were still just puppets in the end.

Feeling as authentic as a psalm on the bumper of a stolen car, with a body in the trunk. Mad eyes flash between rear view and the road ahead bathed in the hunting blue light collage.

Prosecutable philistine performing persecuted plays. Script written on skinned hides; a pen named Hermes molests apemosyne's virgin paper. Repeating truths that refuse to defy a battery of internal interrogation. Do we not tire of being kicked to death by brothers/sisters/neighbours?

The voiceless and disenfranchised lipsync for their life. Historical traditions' roots sprout forth in beautifully progressive ways. Individuality en masse trebuchets the last vestiges of a recently acquired messiah approved state sanctioned discriminatory attacks on divergent, complex personality traits with the hooded lack of accountability, Saville suited cobras spitting poisonous policy. The good luck's all gone. Fucked up it surely is. Ru-vealing vulnerability isn't such a biggie, when the realisation dawns that vulnerability is existential.

Signed meat-caged spiritual being, stardust scarecrow experiencing heaven and hell in human built, godless, technologically driven cities.

The self-saboteur lies in wait in the dark: plunger depressed ready for the sequel.

It's an admission.

# (DIS) HONESTY

Dishonesty is essentially opening doors with a broken skeleton key.

It'll let you into a life:

you don't deserve—or never lived.

Learned from things observed, information sieved.

Stories heard.

Creating creatures from clay.

A golem named 'No One' named this one and that one—illustrating the way you wished you were.

When it's real, you usually wish you weren't. That person. That thing. There at that time or dishing out those things.

Giving people rings that are undeserved. Acting in ways that are truly fucking absurd.

Guess in there is the real crux of it. Either you did it or you didn't. You lived it or you lied. You fought, scraped and held things close you'd never die for. But the truth.

*The truth*

Is usually a ear and a fucking eyesore.

## Wishing Wells & Personal Hells

Conversations unremembered—

would appear a resignation is tendered.

Broken so badly he cannot be mended.

An offender offended, resentment impending.

Mending begins with very careful tending,

bars are raised by resisting re-offending.

Lending weight to words worth *nowt* at all.

He just comes off as condescending.

Comes off as things a lot worse than that.

A ruffian, a blaggard, a deceiver...a twat.

But his nature for petulance and being pissed make for a mid-thirties brat.

Track back through the years overgrown with criminality and crack.

The pictures are a little clearer, he could've been something way meaner. Something way better. Something way cleaner.

But that wasn't the case, just memories erased, dark nights and even darker days. Paved ways to old places, losing kind and caring faces. Replacing adulation with deserved condemnation.

Didn't listen. Couldn't hear. Poked out blurry eyes and hacked off deaf ears.

Don't know this time if the smoke ever clears.

Wishing wells and personal hells are what continue to get him here.

# The Old Beast

Why does it bother me? These little pieces of mental
policy. Applied to a divide between misogyny and
monogamy. I wish I could justify my attitude towards
the thing, as if trust should just be enough then private
numbers ring. Sending me back into the pit, where I just
live in the shit. Remembering to forget about whos and
wheres and what's in the bin.

How do you just end up getting used: to walking your
own home like a crime scene whenever you enter suspect
rooms? Been out for the day or away for the weekend,
opportunity and motive walk around in my skull...I
know someone has been there. Peering over shoulder on
secret socials' surveillance. Stakeouts coincide with
feeling alive, but now there's naught to be found. No car
parked in the drive.

See, it's a strange one to consider. The deeds done and
you've done the deed yourself. Application of MO to the
offender with a behavioural profile matched against
reputation. That said, you know you've done this, you've
also been right before. The set up feels right. I walk in
these paranoid shoes comfortably. Recitation of the
story doesn't lead to finding trust murdered in
photographs on the floor. Creating visions of 'what-ifs'

based on self-esteem issues need to stay with the old beast and its inebriation.

The perp is easy to find in any reflective surface. Manifesting malady of mind based on past presumptions and unusual communication disruptions. Never means the assumptions trump loving another. It simply means they've made you and your investigation can no longer stay undercover. When you've planted evidence and muddied their name, echoes of entrapment and smear campaigns.

Then I just talked to you. Changed the disposition of my view. Explained why I felt the way I felt and how much I wanted those feelings to go away.

Reassurance was everything. Resuscitation for prideful condemnation of the thoughts and feelings founded in the older ways of living. Lives spent with nothing, no care for dignity nor emotion. The old beast always stalks, when I'm alone and you're ~~astray~~ away. A land filled with fidgeting hands and filled ashtrays.

We move: love evolves and stirs into motion. Another letter written on my paranoia, how I overcome it:

All thanks to that person's patience and devotion. I become it.

## SPIRITED & WISTFUL

Furious bluster appears to be about all I can muster.
Creeping, encroaching demons' beckon with goblets and
dusty lustre. Feeling the pressure to sip and slip back
under. I'll need a feeding tube; a bleeding tube and I'll
just be another burnt out medicated blunder.

He's naught but regret, game, set, matched the pace with
all the jockeys. Slinging drinks and spilling ink have
become very tainted hobbies. Parting ways with my old
favourite ways to decay has me wits end, vexed and
sobbing.

When you're pricked by a poison that tests your very
nature to resist. Restricts social movements and days
creep by like

      a       s i n g l e   solitary

                                                inch.


Each day taken is a measure, two fluid ounces or off the
measures.

      I wistfully think of every spirited sitch.

Cartographers couldn't map this degeneration.
Degenerative mental illness parts the tide for this

~~non-~~alc drinking drunk's dreaded dissemination. Repetitive repatriotization to sobrieties nation, that ignores past labels and denotations, can't happen until you really move past the bottle's bittersweet supplication.

Feel it's the root of my creation, the blue-eyed boy breast fed on procrastination, situational and recreational abuse and section two litigation.

How come getting better means feeling worse; this torturous attachment to self-preservation?

I felt way better cursing the world, the kind of oyster who hid his own pearl; then borrowed yours, then I'm out the oceanic back door.

"Never seen that before, Sharky." "No comment, get my brief please, Officer George."

Doesn't take a genius to solve this mystery: crime boss shark's feed on shoals who work their soles and souls 'til they bleed.

Driving chorey Astra's through DH and NE. Coastal postcodes and motorways carrying weight, a set of real jangling keys.

Some days I get up and wage war after fucking war; internally troops are mown down on my entrenched trauma's fortified shore.

Remind me again, why do I actually give a fuck...really give a fuck at all, anymore?

## GIVE A WHAT?

You give a fuck because you're worth it. You give a fuck because you were to blame. You give a fuck because it's all you've got left to give besides the horrid, steadfast heartache and self-loathesome, bottomless shame.

You give a fuck because it's you in the mirror, playing you at your very own game. You give a fuck because you were raised better than that, or because you don't want your kids to grow up the same.

You give a fuck because you voted for this. You give a fuck because war criminals and corruption abound in our fucking name. You give a fuck because your Mam can't afford both heat and to eat. You give a fuck because it's your land yet they tax our homes and our lives from underneath our feet.

You give a fuck because you are the reason that you are here. You give a fuck if you've got a single friend. You give a fuck because you can always make, your situation better. You give a fuck, then life really begins...

You give a fuck because you're worth saving. You give a fuck because plain sailing is easier than pissed-up bus stop complaining. You give a fuck because YOU'RE OUTSIDE and you CAN FEEL THAT it's raining. You give a fuck because it's all that's left when you've dried out, sobered up, and finally remembered 'feeling'. You start by giving a fuck, because then *caring* feels just a little less draining.

## STRENGTH TO STRENGTH

Strength to strength.

Not being strong to being strong.

Feels like literally years since security was felt.

Wolves were either skinned or kept from the door.

An accord can't be struck with a peaceful existence when
subsistence is the only alleyway this rat must run down
to carve out some meek existence.

Lesions in the available balance          next month—

we've     got      to      STEM THE BLEEDING.

Perhaps not for the stress and the streets and its tar pits;
such a beautifully repulsive mess.

Keeps me wondering if this garden of cultivated words
buds in more than the gardener's head?          Rose petal
beds and      suggestively giving head are only one kind of
way to express that which needs said.

Stemming from the hatred/resentment/regret,      it's
not cool to have them,      *I know.*

Come back when you've lived a bit, that's what the
wounds are plugged with at first—

  *Why didn't I stick in and make a nest?*

Keep abreast of being broke and other abusive behaviours, hindsight's waves *crest*.

Sometimes the platter is plated up with all the shit that couldn't be handled     and all the shit that should've been handled, which quickly becomes the shit that leads to flying off the handle. Hiding from     *knock knocks, ring rings,*          letterbox assaults with graded and coloured paper bullets.     Taking shots because the door remains stoic; unanswered and locked.

Could've been so much easier. If only everything was different. Up was down and time moved backward and forward when commanded unbidden. Things didn't happen and other things did.

*Would it be traded in for existence?*

*Surviving to thrive through decline is just life.*

Candles on the mantle burning wicks send waxy stalactites growing beneath—

*the perfect glass clock—*

just waiting to go

*tick.*

*Regret is the thief of time.*

That's what they won't tell you—

the only reason no one admits to it.

# Epilogue

*'Life's a slog, one broken cog, a tendril laden, fog blanketed bog, with witches and heathens and poisonous frogs. Or maybe psychedelic toads, and yellow brick roads, through a wonderful colour-filled paradise: my magical abode. Perhaps, you've got the secret and no key, the you and no me, blind leading blind.'*

Another piece I wrote back in my developmental stages, somewhere around 2012. Before the stabilisers came off and I could free wheel my way to something I considered good writing. This piece above, however, always spoke to me. A lot of bricks went into my yellow brick road...not many were yellow. Not much fucking magic either, nevermind a real, stable abode to call home.

*Magic does exist though.*

Pratchett taught me that. Showed me the *colour of magic.* He created a world in which both me and my father frolicked on damaged legs and nerves through words and situations so precisely crafted and absurd, that the mirror they held up to our own little world was heard on tapes and discs. The only place I'm still always happy to be whisked, whenever the opportunity presents itself to reconvene with Nanny Ogg and Granny Weatherwax.

I think often of both those men. My father, and Sir Terry. Two of the men who influenced me most in my life (and my Grandpa Les, of course).

One gave me something to fear. The other gave me something to aim for. The last gave me everything else.

I suppose, in my own way, I'm still trying to be all of them.

We shall see...

Join us next time for more Husband Material.

*Two generations worth.*

# ABOUT THE AUTHOR

D.L. 'Dan' Husband is a North East UK born poet and writer. His first book 'Stories From The Streets' was published by Dead Man's Press Ink June '24. His first piece of published work was featured in ANARKISS zine in April '24 and there have been many more following including anthology features for Acid Bath Publishing (upcoming), Cozy Ink Press and Bluebird Anthology. These go hand in hand with published work in Sunflower Station Press, PROSETRICS, IceBlinkLit, Prizzie Magazine and a long list for Butcher's dog publishing.

He has also performed at Newcastle Fringe Festival in July '24, with various other spoken word open mics prior and upcoming. He has various regular contributor spots lined up in publications from May '24, including a regular contributor spot for Art Etcetera magazine.

When he is not working in hospitality or spending time with his partner in County Durham, he is hard at work with both pen and page. Right and wrong. This and that...

## Colloquial Glossary

Knaa – know

Wor – our – 'wor kid' means my sibling' or my friend.

Nowt – nothing

Divvn't – don't

Kidder – joker/grifter

Owt – anything

Gannin' – going

Canny – quite/very/nice – 'Gan canny' means calm down. 'Canny bleak' means quite bleak.

Wey – well

Aye – agreement; yes.

Chore/chored/chorey - steal, stealing or stolen.

www.ingramcontent.com/pod-product-compliance
Lightning Source LLC
Chambersburg PA
CBHW020757130626
46554CB00006B/2228